To

_____

From

_____

On the occasion of

_____

A KEEPSAKE JOURNAL FOR THE ONE YOU LOVE

MY SON'S

Blessing Book

WATERBROOK
PRESS

MY SON'S BLESSING BOOK
PUBLISHED BY WATERBROOK PRESS
2375 Telstar Drive, Suite 160
Colorado Springs, Colorado 80920
A division of Random House, Inc.

ISBN 1-57856-431-X

Printed in the United States of America
2001—First Edition

10 9 8 7 6 5 4 3 2 1

The LORD bless you
and keep you;
the LORD make his face shine upon you
and be gracious to you;
the LORD turn his face toward you
and give you peace.

NUMBERS 6:24-26

INTRODUCTION

Our son is a heritage from the Lord. We know this to the depths of our parent souls and are grateful. We store up this gratitude in our hearts, perhaps as Mary did, uncertain but hopeful of what this heritage wrapped up in a young boy's body might promise.

Over the years it will begin to unwrap itself. We will participate in the process: helping, guiding, watching, waiting. And along the way the hope we hold out to our son is apt to have trouble containing itself. Our most difficult task may be the waiting, the waiting for God and our son to do together those things that we can't do for him ourselves.

So while we wait, we love and pray and look for ways to give our son every ounce of wisdom we possess. We want him to know that our love for him is bottomless and that our Lord's love for him is even greater than that. We want to impart to him confidence, joy, strength, Christlikeness, and a long list of other desirable traits as he walks toward manhood. In the depths of our hearts we know he is a temporary resident in our home and will be "ours" for only a brief time. We suspect that one day our son will stand before us and we will find that the waiting has passed like lightning.

In the meantime, we might hope he will forget some of the things we tell him and teach him—things well intentioned but riddled with the shortcomings of our humanness. Other things we hope he will remember forever. Those things are worth writing down.

If we were to do so, we would create a permanent testament for our son to keep, a personalized record of our love and God's as it applies to the details of his existence, a documentation of the physical and spiritual heritage that has unfolded in his life. Whatever might happen to us, whatever route his life might take, he would always have it. He would always be able to read it, always be encouraged by it, ever pointed back, as if by a compass, to the love of Christ and his Father's perfect Word.

This is that record.

Or rather, this will become that record, just as soon as you put your pen to its paper.

How to Use This Book

*Y*our son's *Blessing Book* contains twenty-one sets of pages for entries, each of which is introduced by a scripture. Ultimately, *you* get to decide when and how you want to complete this book for your son. Its flexible format offers several options, a few of which are listed on the following pages.

Pick a realistic approach that suits your desires, abilities, and circumstances. Keep your goals simple. Blessing your son doesn't have to be a flamboyant or spectacular gesture. In fact, the simplest words and briefest messages are often the most meaningful.

Here are some ideas—you may decide to use them all, just a few, or others of your own—to help you in the process:

WHEN SHOULD I WRITE?

One simple option is to write a once-a-year letter to your son on a meaningful annual date, such as his birthday, his "conversion birthday," a holiday, or the first day of each school year. You might give the journal to him each year to keep, taking it back only to write the next entry, or you might wait until he is of a certain age or has entered a particular rite of passage before giving the completed *Blessing Book* to him.

You might decide to write at shorter intervals: weekly, monthly, even daily during a period of time when he especially needs your encouragement. Your entries could be even less ordered than that if you prefer spontaneity. Allow them to be triggered by random events, such as an achievement, a time shared together, a new stage of life, a loss or disappointment, and so on.

Between entries, as you have thoughts but don't have time to write them down in a formal entry, jot short notes in the pages at the back of the *Blessing Book* to remind yourself of what you want to write. Use sticky notes if you run out of space.

WHAT SHOULD I SAY?

Try to keep the content of your entries focused directly on your son. You might:

- Affirm his uniqueness and giftedness, his talents and abilities.
- Reiterate your unconditional love for him.
- Share your hopes and dreams for him.

- Praise specific accomplishments, as well as his growth and maturity.

- Point him to the wisdom of God's Word as he seeks guidance for life.

- Identify a favorite scripture and explain its relevance to his life as you see it.

- Reflect upon the hope and promises contained in one or more of the scriptures in this *Blessing Book.*

- Applaud his efforts to live uprightly.

- Ask forgiveness for an error you've made in parenting him.

- Thank him for specific ways in which he has blessed you.

- Tell stories of events that occurred when he was too young to remember.

- Document events that he will want to remember later and explain why you think they're important.

- Make a list of his traits that you find commendable and praise what is Christlike in him.

- Encourage him during difficult times of trial, grief, disappointment, or waywardness.

- Identify life lessons you've learned and how they have shaped the way you parent him.

- Explain his special place in the family and describe what he contributes to it.

- Recount a special moment you shared with him and explain why you'll never forget it.

If you like, experiment with formats that lend variety to your entries:

- Write down your prayers for him.
- Craft a poem or song for your son, perhaps one easy for him to memorize.
- Retell a favorite story of blessing (or create a new one) with your son as the star.
- Paste favorite photos into the entry pages. Write captions that tell "the rest of the story."
- Press flowers that represent a special place or moment—his birthplace, favorite spot, first date, and so on—between the pages.
- Draw a picture that communicates a thought of blessing to him.

Moms and dads each play a unique role in blessing their sons. Consider taking turns so that your son's *Blessing Book* contains words of love from both of you.

No matter how you decide to fill out this book or how long it takes you to complete it, the resulting blessing to your son will be immeasurable in the years to come. There are some things that only a parent can say, some holes only a parent can fill, some blessings only a parent can give. As you bless your son with the love of our Lord, Christ will bless you richly in return.

*Sons are a heritage from the L*ORD,
children a reward from him.
Like arrows in the hands of a warrior
are sons born in one's youth.

PSALM 127:3-4

Blessed is he
   whose transgressions are forgiven,
   whose sins are covered.
Blessed is the man whose sin the LORD does not
      count against him
   and in whose spirit is no deceit.

PSALM 32:1-2

So we have continued praying for you ever since we first heard about you. We ask God to give you a complete understanding of what he wants to do in your lives, and we ask him to make you wise with spiritual wisdom. Then the way you live will always honor and please the Lord, and you will continually do good, kind things for others. All the while, you will learn to know God better and better. We also pray that you will be strengthened with his glorious power so that you will have all the patience and endurance you need. May you be filled with joy, always thanking the Father, who has enabled you to share the inheritance that belongs to God's holy people, who live in the light.

COLOSSIANS 1:9-12 (NLT)

*Don't let anyone look down on you because you are
young, but set an example for the believers in speech,
in life, in love, in faith and in purity.... Watch your
life and doctrine closely. Persevere in them, because if
you do, you will save both yourself and your hearers.*

1 TIMOTHY 4:12,16

For Thou didst form my inward parts;
Thou didst weave me in my mother's womb.
I will give thanks to Thee, for I am fearfully
  and wonderfully made;
Wonderful are Thy works,
And my soul knows it very well.
My frame was not hidden from Thee,
When I was made in secret,
And skillfully wrought in the depths of the earth.
Thine eyes have seen my unformed substance;
And in Thy book they were all written,
The days that were ordained for me,
When as yet there was not one of them.

PSALM 139:13-16 (NASB)

My son, if you accept my words
   and store up my commands within you,
turning your ear to wisdom
   and applying your heart to understanding,
and if you call out for insight
   and cry aloud for understanding,
and if you look for it as for silver
   and search for it as for hidden treasure,
then you will understand the fear of the LORD
   and find the knowledge of God.
For the LORD gives wisdom,
   and from his mouth come knowledge and understanding.
He holds victory in store for the upright,
   he is a shield to those whose walk is blameless,
for he guards the course of the just
   and protects the way of his faithful ones.
Then you will understand what is right and just
   and fair—every good path.
For wisdom will enter your heart,
   and knowledge will be pleasant to your soul.
Discretion will protect you,
   and understanding will guard you.

PROVERBS 2:1-11

That is why we have a great High Priest who has gone to heaven, Jesus the Son of God. Let us cling to him and never stop trusting him. This High Priest of ours understands our weaknesses, for he faced all of the same temptations we do, yet he did not sin. So let us come boldly to the throne of our gracious God. There we will receive his mercy, and we will find grace to help us when we need it.

HEBREWS 4:14-16 (NLT)

May the LORD answer you when you are in distress;
may the name of the God of Jacob protect you.
May he send you help from the sanctuary
and grant you support from Zion.
May he remember all your sacrifices
and accept your burnt offerings.
May he give you the desire of your heart
and make all your plans succeed.
We will shout for joy when you are victorious
and will lift up our banners in the name of our God.
May the LORD grant all your requests.

PSALM 20:1-5

Endure hardship as discipline; God is treating you as sons. For what son is not disciplined by his father?... [W]e have all had human fathers who disciplined us and we respected them for it. How much more should we submit to the Father of our spirits and live! Our fathers disciplined us for a little while as they thought best; but God disciplines us for our good, that we may share in his holiness. No discipline seems pleasant at the time, but painful. Later on, however, it produces a harvest of righteousness and peace for those who have been trained by it.

HEBREWS 12:7,9-11

Come, my children, and listen to me,
*   and I will teach you to fear the LORD.*
Do any of you want to live
*   a life that is long and good?*
Then watch your tongue!
*   Keep your lips from telling lies!*
Turn away from evil and do good.
*   Work hard at living in peace with others.*

PSALM 34:11-14 (NLT)

DATE: _____

Blessed are the poor in spirit,
  for theirs is the kingdom of heaven.
Blessed are those who mourn,
  for they will be comforted.
Blessed are the meek,
  for they will inherit the earth.
Blessed are those who hunger and thirst for righteousness,
  for they will be filled.
Blessed are the merciful,
  for they will be shown mercy.
Blessed are the pure in heart,
  for they will see God.
Blessed are the peacemakers,
  for they will be called sons of God.
Blessed are those who are persecuted because of righteousness,
  for theirs is the kingdom of heaven.

MATTHEW 5:3-10

*For this reason, I bow my knees before the Father,
from whom every family in heaven and on earth
derives its name, that He would grant you, according
to the riches of His glory, to be strengthened with
power through His Spirit in the inner man; so that
Christ may dwell in your hearts through faith; and
that you, being rooted and grounded in love, may be
able to comprehend with all the saints what is the
breadth and length and height and depth, and to
know the love of Christ which surpasses knowledge,
that you may be filled up to all the fulness of God.*

EPHESIANS 3:14-19 (NASB)

People were bringing little children to Jesus to have him touch them, but the disciples rebuked them. When Jesus saw this, he was indignant. He said to them, "Let the little children come to me, and do not hinder them, for the kingdom of God belongs to such as these. I tell you the truth, anyone who will not receive the kingdom of God like a little child will never enter it." And he took the children in his arms, put his hands on them and blessed them.

MARK 10:13-16

DATE: _____

*If you make the L*ORD *your refuge,*
  if you make the Most High your shelter,
no evil will conquer you;
  no plague will come near your dwelling.
For he orders his angels
  to protect you wherever you go.
They will hold you with their hands
  to keep you from striking your foot on a stone.
You will trample down lions and poisonous snakes;
  you will crush fierce lions and serpents under your feet!
*The L*ORD *says, "I will rescue those who love me.*
  I will protect those who trust in my name.
When they call on me, I will answer;
  I will be with them in trouble.
  I will rescue them and honor them.
I will satisfy them with a long life
  and give them my salvation."

PSALM 91:9-16 (NLT)

Indeed, none of those who wait for Thee will be ashamed;
Those who deal treacherously without cause will be ashamed.
Make me know Thy ways, O LORD;
Teach me Thy paths.
Lead me in Thy truth and teach me,
For Thou art the God of my salvation;
For Thee I wait all the day.
Remember, O LORD, Thy compassion and Thy lovingkindnesses,
For they have been from of old.
Do not remember the sins of my youth or my transgressions;
According to Thy lovingkindness remember Thou me,
For Thy goodness' sake, O LORD.

PSALM 25:3-7 (NASB)

My son, keep your father's commands
  and do not forsake your mother's teaching.
Bind them upon your heart forever;
  fasten them around your neck.
When you walk, they will guide you;
  when you sleep, they will watch over you:
  when you awake, they will speak to you.
For these commands are a lamp,
  this teaching is a light,
and the corrections of discipline are the way to life.

PROVERBS 6:20-23

But because of his great love for us, God, who is rich in mercy, made us alive with Christ even when we were dead in transgressions—it is by grace you have been saved. And God raised us up with Christ and seated us with him in the heavenly realms in Christ Jesus, in order that in the coming ages he might show the incomparable riches of his grace, expressed in his kindness to us in Christ Jesus. For it is by grace you have been saved, through faith—and this not from yourselves, it is the gift of God—not by works, so that no one can boast. For we are God's workmanship, created in Christ Jesus to do good works, which God prepared in advance for us to do.

EPHESIANS 2:4-10

Blessed is the man
  who does not walk in the counsel of the wicked
or stand in the way of sinners
  or sit in the seat of mockers.
But his delight is in the law of the LORD
  and on his law he meditates day and night.
He is like a tree planted by streams of water,
  which yields its fruit in season
and whose leaf does not wither.
  Whatever he does prospers.

PSALM 1:1-3

For the LORD God is a sun and shield;
The LORD gives grace and glory;
No good thing does He withhold
    from those who walk uprightly.

PSALM 84:11 (NASB)

In all my prayers for all of you, I always pray with joy…being confident of this, that he who began a good work in you will carry it on to completion until the day of Christ Jesus…. And this is my prayer: that your love may abound more and more in knowledge and depth of insight, so that you may be able to discern what is best and may be pure and blameless until the day of Christ, filled with the fruit of righteousness that comes through Jesus Christ—to the glory and praise of God.

PHILIPPIANS 1:4,6,9-11

May God himself, the God of peace, sanctify you through and through. May your whole spirit, soul and body be kept blameless at the coming of our Lord Jesus Christ. The one who calls you is faithful and he will do it.

1 THESSALONIANS 5:23-24